TRAVEL GUIDE 2023 - 2024

plus 44 Common Expressions and Phrases to Sound like a Local

PLUS! COMPLIMENTARY
TRAVEL JOURNAL, CHECKLIST & ITINERARY

Sorrento

Travel Guide 2023 - 2024

Your Indispensable Travel Compass and Companion to Explore and Enjoy SORRENTO like never before!

Travel Tips, Tricks & Techniques

Dan L. Allbeta

Table of Content

PREFACE

I'm happy you took a bold step by investing in this one of a kind travel guide (companion and compass). I hope it will be more than a travel guide and perhaps be a dependable travel companion throughout your stay in and around Sorrento.

Welcome to Sorrento, a mesmerizing coastal town nestled in the stunning region of Campania, Italy. With its breathtaking vistas, rich cultural heritage, and tantalizing delicacies, Sorrento beckons travelers from around the globe to indulge in an unforgettable journey of discovery.

As you embark on this travel guide, prepare to immerse yourself in the unique blend of ancient history, vibrant local life, and picturesque landscapes that make Sorrento an unrivaled destination.

Let the adventure begin!

Dan L. Allbeta

"There is a magic in Sorrento that awakens the senses and nourishes the soul."

- Henrik Ibsen

Sorrento at a Glance

Sorrento, a captivating coastal town nestled in the scenic region of Campania, Italy. With its breathtaking vistas, rich history, and mouthwatering cuisine, Sorrento has enthralled travelers for centuries.

Location:

Perched on rugged cliffs overlooking the sparkling waters of the Tyrrhenian Sea, Sorrento is blessed with a stunning setting that will leave you spellbound. Situated in southern Italy, this charming town is easily accessible and serves as an ideal base for exploring the renowned Amalfi Coast and the legendary Isle of Capri.

Natural Beauty:

From its majestic cliffs to the lush countryside, the region offers a feast for the eyes. Wander along the breathtaking Amalfi Coast, a UNESCO World Heritage site, where dramatic cliffs meet the azure sea, and picturesque villages cling to the mountainside. Discover hidden coves, pristine beaches, and vibrant lemon groves..

Historical Significance:

Sorrento carries a rich diversity of history that unfolds as you wander its ancient streets. Founded by the Greeks and later inhabited by the Romans, the town bears the marks of its illustrious past.

Marvel at the architectural marvels that stand as testaments to Sorrento's heritage, such as the awe-inspiring Cathedral and the charming cloisters of Saint Francis. Each stone has a story to tell, and every corner reveals a glimpse into the town's storied past.

Cultural Delights:

Immerse yourself in Sorrento's vibrant local culture, where old traditions blend harmoniously with modern life. Engage with the friendly locals, known for their warm hospitality and zest for life.

Indulge in the lively atmosphere of the town center, where bustling markets, quaint shops, and cozy cafés beckon.

Outdoor Adventures:

If you're seeking outdoor adventures, Sorrento has much to offer. Explore the rugged hiking trails that wind through the lush countryside, offering breathtaking views at every turn.

Embark on boat trips along the dramatic coastline, discovering hidden grottos and pristine beaches. Whether you're an avid hiker, an intrepid explorer, or simply seeking tranquility, Sorrento caters to all.

As you delve into this travel guide, let its pages be your gateway to the wonders of Sorrento. Uncover hidden gems, receive insider tips, and embrace the essence of this enchanting coastal town. Sorrento's natural beauty, rich history, and vibrant culture await your arrival, ready to create memories that will last a lifetime.

"Sorrento, where the sunsets paint the sky in hues of gold, igniting the heart with a sense of wonder."

- Victor Hugo

Chapter 1:
Historical Antecedent of Sorrento

As you set foot in the captivating town of Sorrento, it becomes evident that this place is steeped in a rich tapestry of history that has shaped its very essence.

Sorrento through the Ages

Ancient Origins:

Sorrento is a city with a rich history that dates back over 2,000 years. The first known settlement in the area was founded by the Greeks in the 6th century BC. The Greeks called the city Surreo, which means "flow together." This may refer to the flow of the two ancient rivers that run through the city.

Roman Influences:

The Romans conquered Sorrento in the 3rd century BC, and the city became an important trading port. Sorrento was also a popular destination for Roman artists and poets. The poet Horace wrote about Sorrento in his poems, and the Roman emperor Tiberius had a villa in the city.

Medieval Transformations:

After the fall of the Roman Empire, Sorrento was ruled by a succession of different powers, including the Byzantines, the Lombards, and the Arabs.

In the 11th century, Sorrento became an independent city-state, and it remained so until the 16th century.

Sorrento was then ruled by the Spanish, the Austrians, and the French, before finally becoming part of Italy in the 19th century.

Throughout its history, Sorrento has been a popular destination for travelers, and it is still one of the most popular tourist destinations in Italy today.

Historical Sites To Visit in Sorrento:

- **The Duomo:**

The Duomo is a beautiful cathedral that was built in the 12th century. The cathedral has a rich history, and it is one of the most important religious sites in Sorrento.

- **The Roman Theater:**

The Roman Theater was built in the 1st century BC. The theater is one of the best-preserved Roman theaters in Italy, and it is a popular tourist destination.

- **The Marina Grande:**

The Marina Grande is a picturesque waterfront promenade. The Marina Grande is a great place to walk, people-watch, or take a boat trip to the Isle of Capri.

- **The Piazza Tasso:**

The Piazza Tasso is the main square in Sorrento. The square is named after the famous Italian poet Torquato Tasso, who was born in Sorrento.

The Most Important Historical Events

Here are some of the most important historical events that happened in Sorrento:

- **Founding of Sorrento (6th century BC.):**

Sorrento was founded by the Greeks in the 6th century BC. The Greeks called the city Surreo, which means "flow together."

This may refer to the flow of the two ancient rivers that run through the city.

- **Roman Conquest (3rd century BC):**

The Romans conquered Sorrento in the 3rd century BC. The city became an important trading port, and it was also a popular destination for Roman artists and poets.

The poet Horace wrote about Sorrento in his poems, and the Roman emperor Tiberius had a villa in the city.

- **Middle Ages (11th century):**

After the fall of the Roman Empire, Sorrento was ruled by a succession of different powers, including the Byzantines, the Lombards, and the Arabs. In the 11th century, Sorrento became an independent city-state, and it remained so until the 16th century.

- **Spanish Rule (16th century):**

In the 16th century, Sorrento was conquered by the Spanish. The Spanish ruled the city for over 200 years, and they left a lasting legacy on Sorrento's culture and architecture.

- **Austrian Rule (18th century):**

In the 18th century, Sorrento was conquered by the Austrians. The Austrians ruled the city for over 100 years, before it was finally incorporated into the Kingdom of Italy in 1861.

Modern Era (19th century):

Sorrento has been a popular tourist destination since the 19th century. The city's beautiful scenery, mild climate, and rich history have attracted visitors from all over the world.

"Sorrento is a canvas painted with the colors of joy, where the brushstrokes of nature create masterpieces at every turn."

- Oscar Wilde

Chapter 2:
The Best Time Of The Year To Visit

Sorrento is a popular tourist destination, and there is no bad time to visit. However, there are some times of year that are better than others, depending on what you are looking for in your vacation.

Spring (April-May)

- Mild weather
- Lemons in bloom
- Smaller crowds
- Good time for sightseeing and hiking

Summer (June-August)

- Hot and sunny weather
- Beaches are crowded
- Good time for water sports
- Peak season, so prices are higher

Fall (September-October)

- Warm and sunny weather
- Smaller crowds
- Good time for sightseeing and hiking

Winter (November-March)

- Mild weather
- Fewer tourists
- Good time for shopping and dining
- Some shops and restaurants may close

Ultimately, the best time to visit Sorrento depends on your personal preferences and the experiences you seek. Each season presents its own allure, from the blossoming beauty of spring to the vibrant energy of summer, the enchanting hues of autumn, and the cozy charm of winter.

No matter what time of year you choose to visit Sorrento, you are sure to have a wonderful time.

Choosing Your Perfect Time

Here are some additional factors to consider when deciding when to visit Sorrento:

- **Your budget:**

If you are on a budget, you may want to avoid the peak season (summer).

- **Your interests:**

If you are interested in history and culture, you may want to visit during the spring or fall, when the crowds are smaller.

- **Your activities:**

If you plan on doing a lot of outdoor activities, such as hiking or swimming, you will want to visit during the warmer months.

"In Sorrento, time loses its grip, and the soul finds solace in the eternal beauty that surrounds it."

- Edgar Allan Poe

Chapter 3:
How To Arrive and Move Like a Pro

You can fly into Naples International Airport, which is about 30 kilometers away, or you can take a train from Rome or Naples.

Once you arrive in Sorrento, you can either walk or take a bus to your hotel.

Choosing the Arrival Point:

Sorrento is conveniently located in the Campania region of Italy, offering various options for your arrival.

If you're flying from afar, Naples International Airport is your gateway to Sorrento. With frequent international flights, this airport ensures smooth connectivity from major cities around the world.

Once you land, you'll be just a stone's throw away from your Sorrento adventure.

By Plane

If you are flying into Naples International Airport, you will need to take a bus or taxi to Sorrento. The bus takes about 45 minutes, and the taxi takes about 30 minutes. The bus leaves from the airport every 30 minutes, and the taxi fare is around €25.

By Train

If you are taking a train to Sorrento, you will need to get off at the Sorrento Station. The train station is located in the center of town, so you can easily walk to your hotel from there. The train ride from Rome takes about 2 hours, and the train ride from Naples takes about 30 minutes.

By Bus

There are also several bus companies that offer direct bus service to Sorrento from Naples and Rome. The bus ride from Naples takes about 1 hour, and the bus ride from Rome takes about 3 hours.

Getting Oriented:

As you settle into Sorrento, take a moment to get oriented. The town's central hub is Piazza Tasso, a bustling square filled with cafés, shops, and vibrant energy. From here, you can easily navigate the main streets that radiate outwards, such as Corso Italia and Via San Cesareo.

Sorrento's compact size allows you to navigate its charming corners with ease.

Mastering Local Transportation:

Once you arrive in Sorrento, you will need to find your way to your hotel. If you are walking, you will need to follow the signs to the main square, Piazza Tasso. Your hotel will be located somewhere near the square.

If you are taking a bus or taxi, your hotel will be able to give you directions from the bus or train station.

Here are some additional tips for arriving and landing in Sorrento like a pro:

- Book your flights or train tickets in advance, especially if you are traveling during the peak season.
- Pack comfortable shoes, as you will be doing a lot of walking in Sorrento.
- Bring a camera, as you will want to capture all of the beautiful scenery.
- Learn a few basic Italian phrases, as this will help you communicate with the locals.
- Be prepared for crowds, especially during the peak season.

"Sorrento is a love affair with life, where every moment is infused with passion and the spirit of la dolce vita."

- Elizabeth Gilbert

Chapter 4:
Culture and Tradition of Sorrento

Sorrento, where time-honored culture and vibrant traditions form the beating heart of this coastal gem.

In this chapter, we invite you to immerse yourself in the rich diversity of Sorrento's cultural heritage, where ancient customs and local traditions intertwine to create a captivating experience for every traveler.

Artistic Expressions:

Sorrento has long been a haven for artists, poets, and creative souls drawn to its breathtaking landscapes and timeless beauty. The town's artistic heritage is evident in its vibrant art scene, with galleries showcasing works inspired by the local surroundings.

You'll find yourself captivated by paintings that capture the vibrant colors of the Amalfi Coast, sculptures that pay homage to the town's history, and crafts that embody the essence of Sorrento's craftsmanship.

Musical Melodies:

Music permeates the air of Sorrento, filling its streets and squares with harmonious melodies. The region boasts a rich musical tradition, ranging from traditional folk tunes to classical compositions.

During your visit, you may encounter local musicians serenading passersby with the sweet sounds of mandolins, guitars, and accordions. The melodies of Sorrento will undoubtedly resonate in your heart long after your departure.

Culinary Delights:

Sorrento's culinary scene is a treasure trove of mouthwatering delights. From the zesty notes of freshly squeezed lemonade to the tantalizing aromas of freshly baked pastries, the town's cuisine showcases the region's bountiful produce and rich flavors.

Indulge in the famous limoncello liqueur crafted from Sorrento's lemons, savor the delicate flavors of handmade pasta dishes, and let the savory seafood creations transport you to culinary bliss.

Festivals and Celebrations:

Sorrento's calendar is marked by lively festivals and traditional celebrations that reflect the town's deep-rooted cultural heritage.

One of the most renowned events is the Sorrento Summer Music Festival, where world-class musicians enchant audiences with their performances against the backdrop of Sorrento's stunning scenery.

The Feast of Sant'Antonino, the town's patron saint, is another cherished celebration filled with processions, music, and joyous festivities that honor Sorrento's spiritual traditions.

Local Crafts and Souvenirs:

Exploring Sorrento's narrow streets will reveal a myriad of artisan workshops where time-honored crafts are practiced with passion and precision.

From intricate woodwork and exquisite ceramics to delicate lacework and handmade sandals, these skilled artisans preserve and showcase Sorrento's proud craftsmanship.

Take a piece of Sorrento's cultural heritage home with you by selecting a unique and authentic souvenir crafted by these talented locals.

Architectural Masterpiece

Sorrento's architecture is a mix of styles, reflecting the city's long and varied history. The city's most famous landmark is the Duomo, a beautiful cathedral that was built in the 12th century. The Duomo is a mix of Romanesque and Gothic styles, and it is one of the most important religious sites in Sorrento.

Other notable architectural landmarks in Sorrento include the Marina Grande, a picturesque waterfront promenade; the Piazza Tasso, the main square in Sorrento; and the ruins of the Roman Theater, which was built in the 1st century BC.

Warm Hospitality:

Perhaps the most cherished aspect of Sorrento's culture is the warm hospitality of its residents. The locals, known as "Sorrentini," welcome visitors with open arms and an authentic warmth that instantly makes you feel at home.

Engage in conversations with the friendly locals, exchange smiles, and embrace the genuine camaraderie that permeates the town. Sorrento's hospitality will leave an everlasting impression on your heart.

So, as you wander through Sorrento's captivating streets and embrace its vibrant cultural scene, allow yourself to be immersed in the traditions, artistry, and warmth of this coastal gem.

Important Dates and Celebrations in Sorrento

Here are some of the most important dates and celebrations in Sorrento:

- **Feast of the Madonna del Carmine:**

This religious festival takes place on July 16th and is dedicated to the Madonna del Carmine, the patron saint of Sorrento. The festival features a procession of the Madonna del Carmine statue through the streets of Sorrento, as well as fireworks and other festivities.

- **Lemon Festival:**

This festival celebrates the city's lemons, which are a famous local product. The festival takes place in May and features a variety of events, including lemon tastings, cooking demonstrations, and street performances.

- **Passion Week:**

This religious festival commemorates the Passion of Christ. The festival takes place in the week leading up to Easter and features a number of processions and other events.

- **Sant'Antonino Day:**

This festival celebrates the city's patron saint, Sant'Antonino. The festival takes place on September 16th and features a procession of Sant'Antonino's statue through the streets of Sorrento, as well as fireworks and other festivities.

- **Carnevale di Sorrento:**

This carnival takes place in February and is a fun and festive event. The streets of Sorrento are filled with people dressed up in costumes, and there are parades, concerts, and other events.

- **Sorrento Film Festival:**

This film festival takes place in September and features a selection of Italian and international films. The festival is held in the historic center of Sorrento, and it is a great opportunity to see some of the best films from around the world.

"The beauty of Sorrento is like a gentle melody that lingers in the heart, filling it with harmony and joy."

- Ralph Waldo Emerson

Chapter 5:
Accommodation in Sorrento

When it comes to finding the perfect place to stay in Sorrento, you're in for a treat. This coastal town offers a wide range of accommodations to suit your preferences, from luxurious hotels to cozy bed and breakfasts.

In this chapter, we'll guide you through the diverse options available, ensuring that you find the ideal haven to relax.

Luxurious Retreats:

If you're seeking a pampering experience, Sorrento boasts a selection of luxurious hotels that will exceed your expectations. These elegant retreats offer impeccable service, breathtaking views, and an array of upscale amenities.

From five-star properties with lavish spas and infinity pools overlooking the sea to historic villas transformed into opulent resorts, these accommodations provide an exquisite blend of comfort and sophistication.

10 Best Hotels in Sorrento

1. Hotel Bellevue Syrene

Rating: 5-star

Description: This luxurious hotel offers breathtaking views of the Bay of Naples and Mount Vesuvius. With elegant rooms, a rooftop pool, and a private beach, it exudes timeless charm and sophistication.

Website: www.bellevue.it

Contact: +39 081 878 1024

Price Range: $400-$900 per night

Offers: Spa treatments, gourmet dining experiences

2. Grand Hotel Excelsior Vittoria

Rating: 5-star

Description: Set amidst lush gardens, this historic hotel provides a refined retreat. With spacious rooms, a swimming pool overlooking the sea, and impeccable service, it embodies elegance and tranquility.

Website: https://excelsiorvittoria.com/

Contact: +39 081 877 7111

Price Range: $500-$1,200 per night

Offers: Complimentary breakfast, access to a private beach club

3. **Hotel Antiche Mura**

Rating: 4-star

Description: Located in the heart of Sorrento, this charming hotel blends classic elegance with modern comforts. Its rooftop terrace offers panoramic views, and the attentive staff ensures a memorable stay.

Website: www.hotelantichemura.com

Contact: +39 081 807 3599

Price Range: $200-$400 per night

Offers: Free Wi-Fi, guided tours, cooking classes

4. **Hotel Continental**

Rating: 4-star

Description: This family-run hotel combines contemporary design with warm hospitality. Located near Piazza Tasso, it offers comfortable rooms, a rooftop pool, and a renowned restaurant serving local cuisine.

Website: https://www.continentalsorrento.com/en

Contact: +39 081 878 2025

Price Range: $250-$500 per night

Offers: Complimentary shuttle service, fitness center

5. **Hotel Mediterraneo Sorrento**

Rating: 4-star

Description: Situated on a cliffside, this hotel offers breathtaking views of the Gulf of Naples. With its Mediterranean-style rooms, panoramic terrace, and pool, it provides a peaceful and scenic retreat.

Website: www.mediterraneosorrento.com

Contact: +39 081 878 1101

Price Range: $150-$350 per night

Offers: Complimentary breakfast, shuttle service to town center

6. **Hotel La Favorita**

Rating: 4-star

Description: Located near the historic center, this boutique hotel boasts stylish rooms and a rooftop terrace with panoramic views. It offers personalized service and a central location for exploring Sorrento.

Website: www.hotellafavorita.com

Contact: +39 081 878 2207

Price Range: $200-$400 per night

Offers: Wine tastings, cooking demonstrations

7. Grand Hotel La Pace

Rating: 4-star

Description: Nestled in a tranquil park, this hotel offers a serene atmosphere and luxurious amenities. With spacious rooms, a pool, and a wellness center, it provides a serene escape from the bustling town.

Website: http://www.grandhotellapace.it/en/

Contact: +39 081 878 4590

Price Range: $300-$600 per night

Offers: Spa treatments, complimentary shuttle service

8. Hotel Tramontano Sorrento

Rating: 4-star

Description: Perched on a cliff overlooking the Marina Grande, this historic hotel offers panoramic sea views.

With its classic décor, charming rooms, and seaside terrace, it exudes old-world charm.

Website: www.hoteltramontanosorrento.com

Contact: +39 081 878 2422

Price Range: $250-$500 per night

Offers: Boat excursions, private beach access

9. Hotel Bristol

Rating: 3-star

Description: Located in the heart of Sorrento, this hotel offers comfortable rooms and a welcoming atmosphere. Its central location makes it an ideal base for exploring the town's attractions.

Contact: +39 081 878 4522

Price Range: $150-$300 per night

Offers: Rooftop terrace, complimentary breakfast

10. Hotel Rivage

Rating: 3-star

Description: Situated near the beach, this family-run hotel provides a cozy and friendly atmosphere.

With comfortable rooms, a sun terrace, and proximity to the town center, it offers a relaxed stay.

Website: www.rivage.it

Contact: +39 081 878 1873

Price Range: $100-$250 per night

Offers: Beach access, bicycle rentals

Bed and Breakfasts:

If you prefer a more intimate and homely setting, Sorrento has a range of quaint bed and breakfasts that will make you feel like a part of the local community.

These cozy accommodations offer comfortable rooms, often adorned with traditional furnishings, and homemade breakfasts that showcase the flavors of the region. The warm and welcoming hosts provide insider tips and recommendations, making your stay in Sorrento even more memorable.

Top 3 B&B in Sorrento

1. Vista Mare B&B Sorrento

Vista Mare B&B sits near the port and a short drive from Corso Italia. Guests can easily reach Sorrento city center within a 5-minute walk. The surrounding area is filled with restaurants and bars, ensuring a variety of dining options.

Facilities: Safe deposit box, VIP check-in/ -out, 24-hour security, locker room, housekeeping, WiFi

Rating: 4.9/5.0

2. Magnifico B&B Sorrento

The accommodation is conveniently situated near Piazza Lauro and only 180 meters away from Sorrento Circumvesuviana railway station. You'll find yourself just 0.8 km away from the public beach of Sorrent.

Facilities: Paid airport shuttle, Hiking, Cycling, Sports trainer, Free Wi-Fi in rooms, Safe deposit box, 24-hour reception, Luggage storage, Housekeeping, Car hire.

Rating: 4.9/5.0

3. Casa Rosetta Bed & Breakfast

This B&B sits conveniently close to Piazza Tasso, a mere 5-minute stroll from Sorrento Circumvesuviana train station. It is located approximately a 6-minute walk from Via Marina Piccola and about 1 km from Sedile Dominova.

Facilities: WiFi, Shared kitchen, Electric kettle, Cookware/ Kitchen utensils, Outdoor dining area, Air conditioning, Heating, Sitting area, Terrace, Garden furniture, Tea and coffee facilities, Dining table

Rating: 4.0/5.0

Family-Friendly Options:

If you're traveling with little ones, Sorrento have you covered with family-friendly accommodations that cater to the needs of both children and adults. These accommodations offer spacious rooms or suites, dedicated play areas, and services tailored to families, ensuring a comfortable and enjoyable stay for everyone.

Apartments:

Apartments are a good option for families or groups of friends. Apartments in Sorrento typically have kitchens, so you can save money by cooking your own meals.

- **Sorrento Apartments**

Sorrento Apartments is a residential complex strategically positioned in the historical center of Sorrento, a mere one hundred meters away from the sea.

Within minutes, you can explore the ancient path of Roman-origin orthogonal streets and immerse yourself in the captivating charm of history.

Along this path, you will encounter notable landmarks such as the neogothic Cathedral dating back to the fifteenth century and the Arabic San Francesco cloister. Your journey will eventually lead you to the central Piazza Tasso, a significant gathering place for the locals.

Contact: 009 39 081 878 1425

Website: https://www.sorrentoapartments.com/

Rating: 4.5/5.0

Villas:

Villas are a great option for you if you a luxurious and private stay. Villas in Sorrento often have stunning views, and they can accommodate large groups.

- **Villa Acampora**

Villa Acampora is a luxurious and stylish villa situated on the hills of Sorrento. From this vantage point, you can marvel at the breathtaking views of the bay of Naples, Vesuvius, and the Sorrento Peninsula. The villa offers 5 spacious bedrooms, 5 luxurious bathrooms, a private swimming pool, large terraces with sea views, a private garden, air conditioning, Wi-Fi, and parking.

Villa Acampora is the ideal sanctuary for small groups or families seeking the epitome of luxury and style for their getaway in Sorrento.

Rating: 4.5/5.0

Budget-Friendly Options:

If you are vacating in Sorrento on a budget, Sorrento offers a variety of affordable accommodations that provide comfort without breaking the bank. These budget-friendly options include guesthouses, hostels, and smaller hotels that prioritize affordability without compromising on cleanliness and comfort.

These establishments allow you to experience Sorrento's charm while keeping your expenses in check.

Hotels

- **Hotel Mignon:**

This 2-star hotel is located in the heart of Sorrento, just a short walk from the Piazza Tasso. It has a simple but comfortable rooms, and it offers free breakfast and Wi-Fi.

Contact: 009 39 081 807 3824

Website: https://www.sorrentohotelmignon.com/

Rating: 4.5/5.0

Bed and Breakfast

Bed and Breakfast Il Cavatappi:

This family-run bed and breakfast is located in a quiet neighborhood just outside of the city center. It has charming rooms, and it offers a delicious breakfast made with fresh local ingredients.

Rating: 4.2/5.0

Apartments

- **Apartments in the Marina Grande:**

There are many apartments available for rent in the Marina Grande, Sorrento's waterfront district. These apartments are a great option for families or groups of friends, and they often have balconies with stunning views of the Bay of Naples

Mid-range Options

Hotels

- **Hotel Antiche Mura:**

This 4-star hotel is located in the historic center of Sorrento, within walking distance of the Piazza Tasso and the Duomo. It has stylish rooms, and it offers a rooftop terrace with panoramic views of the city and the sea.

Rating: 5.0/5.0 (based on previous occupants' reviews)

- **Hotel Poseidon:**

This 4-star hotel is located on the cliffs overlooking the Bay of Naples. It has luxurious rooms, and it offers a spa, a fitness center, and a rooftop pool with stunning views.

Contact: +39 089 81 11 11

Email: info@hotelposeidonpositano.it

Website: https://www.hotelposeidonpositano.it/

Villas

- **Villas in the hills above Sorrento:**

There are many villas available for rent in the hills above Sorrento. These villas offer stunning views of the city and the sea, and they are a great option for those who want a more secluded and luxurious stay.

Luxury Options:

Hotels

- **Grand Hotel Excelsior Vittoria:**

This 5-star hotel is located on the cliffs overlooking the Bay of Naples. It has opulent rooms, and it offers a spa, a fitness center, and a rooftop pool with stunning views.

Contact: +39 081 877 7111

Email: info@exvitt.it

Website: https://excelsiorvittoria.com/index.html

Rating: 4.7/5.0

- **Hotel Royal Continental:**

This 5-star hotel is located in the heart of Sorrento, just a short walk from the Piazza Tasso.

It has elegant rooms, and it offers a spa, a fitness center, and a rooftop terrace with panoramic views of the city and the sea.

Contact: +39 081 807 2608

Email: info@continentalsorrento.com

Website: https://www.continentalsorrento.com/en

Rating: 4.6/5.0

- **Grand Hotel Santa Caterina:**

This 5-star hotel is located on the cliffs overlooking the Bay of Naples. It has lavish rooms, and it offers a spa, a fitness center, and a private beach with stunning views.

Contact: +39 089 871012

Email: info@hotelsantacaterina.it

Website: https://www.hotelsantacaterina.it/en/home/

Rating: 4.7/5.0

4 Keys to Choose a Suitable Accommodation

Here are some additional tips for choosing accommodation in Sorrento:

1. **Book** your accommodation in advance, especially if you are traveling during the peak season.
2. **Read reviews** of different accommodation options before you book.
3. **Consider the location** of your accommodation. If you want to be close to the action, you may want to choose a hotel in the center of Sorrento. If you prefer a more peaceful stay, you may want to choose an accommodation option in the hills.
4. **Ask about discounts.** Many hotels and other accommodation providers offer discounts for longer stays or for bookings made in advance.

Chapter 6:
Must-See Attraction Spots in Sorrento

In the enchanting town of Sorrento, there are numerous must-see attractions that will leave you spellbound.

This chapter will guide you through the most captivating spots in Sorrento, ensuring that you don't miss out on these remarkable experiences during your visit.

Piazza Tasso:

Located in the heart of Sorrento, Piazza Tasso is a vibrant square bustling with life. Take a leisurely stroll through the charming streets that surround it, and immerse yourself in the lively atmosphere. Sit at a café, sip on an espresso, and watch the world go by.

The central location of Piazza Tasso makes it an ideal starting point for exploring Sorrento's delights.

Marina Grande:

Head to Marina Grande, a picturesque fishing village nestled on the waterfront. This idyllic spot offers a glimpse into Sorrento's coastal charm. Stroll along the promenade, admire the colorful houses, and indulge in fresh seafood at one of the charming restaurants.

With its laid-back atmosphere and stunning views, Marina Grande is a must-visit destination.

Villa Comunale:

Escape to the tranquility of Villa Comunale, a beautiful park overlooking the sea. This lush oasis invites you to relax amidst the verdant gardens, take a leisurely walk along the scenic paths, and enjoy panoramic views of the Bay of Naples.

The fragrant flowers, well-manicured lawns, and refreshing sea breeze create a serene ambiance, providing a perfect respite from the bustling streets.

Cloister of San Francesco:

Step back in time and explore the Cloister of San Francesco, a hidden gem within Sorrento's historic center. This 14th-century cloister features stunning architectural details, including intricately carved columns and elegant arches.

Take a moment to appreciate the serene courtyard, adorned with lush greenery and fragrant orange trees. The cloister's peaceful atmosphere offers a serene retreat from the outside world.

Sorrento Cathedral:

Make your way to Sorrento Cathedral, a magnificent structure that showcases a blend of architectural styles. Marvel at the intricate facade and step inside to admire the stunning frescoes, marble sculptures, and ornate decorations.

The cathedral's beauty and historical significance make it a noteworthy landmark in Sorrento.

Corso Italia:

Embark on a shopping spree along Corso Italia, Sorrento's main shopping street. This bustling thoroughfare is lined with a diverse array of shops, boutiques, and artisan workshops.

Explore the local stores, where you'll find handmade crafts, limoncello, fashionable clothing, and unique souvenirs to take home. Indulge in some retail therapy and soak up the lively ambiance of this vibrant street.

Sedile Dominova:

Discover the historical significance of Sedile Dominova, an impressive 15th-century building that served as a meeting place for Sorrento's noble families. Admire its elegant architecture and detailed carvings, and imagine the gatherings and events that took place within its walls.

Today, it stands as a testament to Sorrento's rich cultural heritage.

"Sorrento's cuisine is a celebration of flavors, where each dish tells a story of the region's rich culinary heritage."

- Julia Child

Chapter 7:
Food and Drink

Sorrento is a haven for food enthusiasts, offering a delightful array of culinary delights and traditional flavors. In this chapter, we invite you to embark on a gastronomic journey, exploring the rich and diverse food and drink scene that Sorrento has to offer.

Traditional Cuisine:

Indulge in the authentic flavors of Sorrento's traditional cuisine, which showcases the region's fresh and high-quality ingredients.

Sample dishes such as "Gnocchi alla Sorrentina" - potato dumplings in a rich tomato sauce with melted mozzarella, or "Linguine ai Frutti di Mare" - linguine pasta with an abundance of fresh seafood.

Don't miss the opportunity to savor the famous "Limoncello" liqueur, made from Sorrento's luscious lemons.

Seafood Delicacies:

Given its coastal location, Sorrento is renowned for its delectable seafood. Delight in dishes such as "Spaghetti alle Vongole" - spaghetti with clams, or "Frittura di Paranza" - a mixed fried seafood platter.

These dishes showcase the freshness of the Mediterranean catch and are sure to tantalize your taste buds. Pair them with a chilled glass of local white wine for a truly memorable dining experience.

Pizzerias and Trattorias:

Sorrento is home to numerous pizzerias and trattorias that serve mouthwatering pizzas and hearty traditional dishes. Relish a slice of Neapolitan-style pizza, topped with fresh ingredients and baked in a wood-fired oven.

Explore trattorias tucked away in narrow streets, offering homemade pasta, succulent meats, and flavorful sauces. These family-run establishments provide an authentic taste of Sorrento's culinary heritage.

Gelato and Pastries:

Satisfy your sweet tooth with a visit to Sorrento's gelaterias and pastry shops. Indulge in artisanal gelato, available in a variety of flavors ranging from classic to innovative combinations. Treat yourself to pastries such as "Sfogliatelle" - delicate flaky pastries filled with sweet ricotta cream, or "Baba al Limoncello" - a sponge cake soaked in Limoncello liqueur.

These delectable treats are perfect for a midday pick-me-up or a post-dinner delight.

Wine and Aperitivos:

Immerse yourself in Sorrento's vibrant social scene by enjoying a glass of local wine or an aperitivo. Visit wine bars and enotecas to discover the region's excellent wines, including the renowned Lacryma Christi, made from grapes grown on the slopes of Mount Vesuvius.

Sip on a refreshing Aperol Spritz or Negroni while enjoying the lively ambiance of Sorrento's bars and lounges.

Cooking Classes and Food Tours:

If you're eager to delve deeper into Sorrento's culinary culture, consider joining a cooking class or food tour. Learn to prepare traditional dishes under the guidance of local chefs, exploring the techniques and secrets behind Sorrento's flavors.

Embark on a guided food tour to discover hidden gems, local markets, and the opportunity to sample a variety of culinary delights.

5 Must Taste Cuisine in Sorrento

- **Spaghetti alla Nerano:** This pasta dish is made with zucchini, tomatoes, and garlic, and it is a local specialty.

- **Gnocchi alla Sorrentina:** This pasta dish is made with gnocchi, tomatoes, and mozzarella cheese, and it is another local specialty.

- **Torta Caprese:** This cake is made with chocolate, almonds, and lemons, and it is a delicious and refreshing dessert.

- **Sfogliatelle:** These pastries are made with a thin pastry dough filled with ricotta cheese, and they are a popular snack or dessert.

4 Tips For Finding The Best Food and Drinks

Here are some tips for finding the best food and drinks in Sorrento:

1. **Ask your hotel** or hostel for recommendations.
2. **Explore the local** markets and shops.
3. **Follow** the locals.
4. **Don't be afraid** to try something new.

With its delicious food and drinks, Sorrento is a city that is sure to tantalize your taste buds.

Cafes and Restaurants for All Budgets

There are many amazing cafes and restaurants to choose from, catering to all budgets. Here are a few of the best:

Budget-friendly:

- **Bar Turi:**

This small cafe is a great place to grab a coffee and a pastry. The pastries are made fresh daily, and the coffee is strong and delicious.

- **Caffe Gambrinus:**

This cafe is a Sorrento institution, and it has been serving up delicious food and drinks for over 100 years. The menu features traditional Italian dishes, with reasonable prices.

Contact: +39 081 417582

Rating: 4.1/5.0

- **La Creperie:**

This creperie is a great place to go for a sweet or savory crepe. The crepes are made fresh to order, and the ingredients are high quality.

Mid-range:

- **Ristorante Il Cavatappi:**

This restaurant serves traditional Italian cuisine in a charming setting. The menu features pasta dishes, seafood dishes, and pizzas.

Contact: +39 0341 815349

Website: http://www.cavatappivarenna.it/

- **La Sponda:**

This restaurant has a beautiful location right on the waterfront. The menu features seafood dishes, pasta dishes, and grilled meats. The views are amazing, and the service is excellent.

Website: https://sirenuse.it/en/la-sponda-restaurant/

- **Terrazza Bosquet:**

This restaurant has a rooftop terrace with stunning views of the Bay of Naples. The menu features seafood dishes, pasta dishes, and pizzas. The service is excellent, and the atmosphere is romantic.

Website: https://terrazzabosquet.exvitt.it/en/

Luxury:

- **Il Cavatappi:**

This Michelin-starred restaurant serves modern Italian cuisine in a luxurious setting. The menu features tasting menus, and the ingredients are sourced from the best local producers. The service is impeccable.

- **Il San Pietro:**

This restaurant has a beautiful location right on the cliffs overlooking the Bay of Naples. The menu features seafood dishes, pasta dishes, and grilled meats. The views are amazing, and the service is excellent.

Contact: +39 089 812080

Email: info@ilsanpietro.it

Website: www.ilsanpietro.it

- **Le Sirenuse:**

This luxurious hotel also has a Michelin-starred restaurant. The menu features modern Italian cuisine, and the ingredients are sourced from the hotel's own garden. The wine list is extensive, and the service is impeccable.

"Sorrento is a poem written by nature, where the verses are the waves that caress its shores."

- Gustave Flaubert

Chapter 8:
Recreational and Fun Activities

Sorrento is not only a destination of beauty and culture but also a haven for recreational and fun activities.

In this chapter, we invite you to explore the exciting range of experiences that Sorrento has to offer, catering to all budgets and ensuring an unforgettable vacation for every traveler.

Beaches and Coastal Exploration:

Sorrento's stunning coastline beckons visitors to indulge in beachside relaxation and coastal exploration.

Whether you prefer the sandy shores of Marina Grande or the hidden coves of Marina di Puolo, Sorrento offers an array of beaches to suit every taste.

Bask in the Mediterranean sun, take refreshing dips in crystal-clear waters, or embark on a scenic coastal hike to discover hidden gems along the shoreline.

Boat Tours and Cruises:

Embark on a boat tour or cruise to fully immerse yourself in the coastal beauty of Sorrento. From leisurely sailing trips along the Sorrento Peninsula to exhilarating speedboat adventures to Capri or the Amalfi Coast, there are options to suit every budget.

Marvel at the breathtaking views of towering cliffs, secluded bays, and sparkling turquoise waters. This is an opportunity to create lifelong memories and experience the beauty of the region from a different perspective.

Hiking and Nature Trails:

Sorrento's surroundings provide ample opportunities for hiking and nature enthusiasts. Lace up your hiking boots and explore the trails that wind through the lush countryside.

Venture into the nearby hills, such as the Punta Campanella Natural Reserve, or discover the breathtaking beauty of the Valle delle Ferriere Nature Reserve.

Cooking Classes and Culinary Experiences:

Immerse yourself in the culinary delights of Sorrento through cooking classes and culinary experiences. Learn to prepare traditional Italian dishes under the guidance of local chefs, who will teach you the secrets of authentic flavors.

Visit local farms and wineries to taste regional delicacies, such as olive oil, cheese, and wines. These experiences offer a hands-on approach to understanding Sorrento's gastronomic heritage while allowing you to create and savor delicious meals.

Cultural Excursions and Guided Tours:

Explore the rich cultural heritage of Sorrento through guided tours and excursions. Visit historical sites such as the ancient ruins of Pompeii and Herculaneum, or take a guided tour of the charming villages along the Amalfi Coast.

Discover the history, art, and traditions of Sorrento through visits to museums, cathedrals, and local artisan workshops. These immersive experiences provide insights into the region's past while showcasing its vibrant present.

Shopping and Local Markets:

Indulge in retail therapy and immerse yourself in the local culture by exploring the vibrant markets and boutique shops of Sorrento. Wander through the lively streets lined with shops selling handmade ceramics, limoncello, and local crafts.

Visit the bustling marketplaces, such as the Piazza Tasso or the Sorrento Fish Market, where you can discover fresh produce, spices, and local specialties.

These shopping experiences allow you to take a piece of Sorrento's charm and craftsmanship home with you.

The 10 Best Things To Do In Sorrento

1. Explore the city's historic center.

Sorrento's historic center is a UNESCO World Heritage Site, and it is full of narrow streets, charming squares, and beautiful churches. You can easily spend a few hours wandering around and exploring the area.

2. Visit the Villa Comunale.

This public park is located on the cliffs overlooking the Bay of Naples, and it is a great place to relax and enjoy the views. The park is home to a variety of flowers, trees, and fountains, and it is a great place to take a walk, have a picnic, or just relax and enjoy the views.

3. Take a walk along the Marina Grande.

The Marina Grande is the waterfront district in Sorrento, and it is a great place to find seafood restaurants, shops, and boat tours. The Marina is also a great place to take in the views of the Bay of Naples.

4. Visit the Lemon Groves.

Sorrento is famous for its lemon groves, and there are many opportunities to see these beautiful trees. You can visit the lemon groves on foot, or you can take a boat tour that will take you through the groves.

5. Go hiking in the hills.

There are many different hiking trails located in the hills above Sorrento. These trails offer stunning views of the city and the sea, and they are a great way to get some exercise.

6. Visit the Museum Correale di Terranova.

This museum houses a collection of art and artifacts from the region of Campania. Admission is €5 for adults and €3 for children.

7. Take a cooking class.

There are many different cooking classes available in Sorrento. These classes are a great way to learn about Italian cuisine and to try some delicious food.

8. Attend a concert or performance.

There are many different concerts and performances held in Sorrento throughout the year. These events are a great way to experience the city's vibrant culture.

9. Go sailing.

There are many different sailing tours available in Sorrento. These tours range in price from €50 to €100 per person.

10. Take a boat tour of the Bay of Naples.

There are many different boat tours available that will take you around the Bay of Naples. These tours range in price from €30 to €50 per person.

The 10 Best Romantic Getaways for Couples in Sorrento

1. Stay at a luxurious hotel.

There are many luxurious hotels located in Sorrento. These hotels offer stunning views, excellent service, and fine dining. This is a great way to spoil your loved one and create memories that will last a lifetime.

2. Have a private boat tour of the Bay of Naples.

You can hire a private boat for €200 per hour. This is a great way to explore the Bay of Naples at your own pace, and you can even have the boat decorated with flowers and champagne.

3. Go on a hot air balloon ride.

This is a truly unique and unforgettable experience. You will get to see the Bay of Naples from a bird's eye view, and it is a great way to create memories that will last a lifetime.

4. Visit the Island of Capri.

Capri is a beautiful island located just off the coast of Sorrento. It is a great place to go for a day trip or a longer vacation. The island is known for its stunning scenery, its luxury hotels, and its high-end boutiques.

5. A romantic dinner at a Michelin-starred restaurant.

There are several Michelin-starred restaurants located in Sorrento. These restaurants offer an unforgettable dining experience, and they are a great way to celebrate your love.

6. Stay at a charming B&B.

There are many charming B&Bs located in Sorrento. These B&Bs offer a more intimate and personal experience than large hotels, it's a great way to connect with your loved one.

7. **Take a boat tour of the Amalfi Coast.**

The Amalfi Coast is one of the most beautiful coastlines in the world, and it is a great place to take a boat tour with your loved one. You will get to see some amazing scenery, and you can even stop to swim in the crystal-clear waters.

8. Attend a concert or performance.

There are many different concerts and performances held in Sorrento throughout the year. These events are a great way to experience the city's vibrant culture, and they can be a lot of fun to attend with your loved one.

9. Have a picnic in the Villa Comunale.

The Villa Comunale is a beautiful public park in Sorrento, and it is a great place to have a picnic with your loved one. The park is home to a variety of flowers, trees, and fountains, and it is a great place to relax and enjoy the outdoors.

10. Visit the Lemon Groves.

Sorrento is famous for its lemon groves, and there are many opportunities to see these beautiful trees. You can visit the lemon groves on foot, or you can take a boat tour that will take you through the groves. This is a great way to spend a relaxing afternoon together, and you can even pick some lemons to take home as a souvenir.

Chapter 9: Shopping Activities in Sorrento

There are many different shopping districts to choose from, catering to all budgets.

Budget-friendly:

- **Visit the flea market in Piazza Tasso.**

This flea market is a great place to find souvenirs, clothing, and other items at a bargain price. It is open every Sunday morning.

- **Explore the local markets.**

There are many local markets in Sorrento where you can find fresh produce, cheeses, meats, and other local delicacies. These markets are a great place to experience the local culture and to find some unique souvenirs.

- **Go window shopping in the Via San Cesareo.**

This pedestrian street is home to many high-end shops, but you can also find some more affordable stores. It is a great place to wander around and see the latest fashions.

- **Visit the craft shops in the Centro Storico.**

The Centro Storico is the historic center of Sorrento, and it is home to many craft shops where you can find handmade souvenirs, jewelry, and other items.

Mid-range:

- **Visit the Galleria Umberto I.**

This arcade is a beautiful example of 19th-century architecture, and it is home to many high-end shops. It is a great place to do some serious shopping.

- **Go to a luxury department store.**

There are a few luxury department stores in Sorrento where you can find high-end clothing, jewelry, and other items. This is a great place to splurge on a special occasion.

Luxury:

- **Visit the boutiques in the Via Camerelle.**

This street is home to some of the most exclusive boutiques in Sorrento. You will find designer clothing, jewelry, and other items from all over the world.

"Sorrento, the land of lemons and orange blossoms, where the sweet scents mingle with the sea breeze."

- Enrico Caruso

Chapter 10: Language and Communication

When visiting Sorrento, effective communication can greatly enhance your travel experience. In this chapter, we will guide you through the language and communication aspects to ensure you have a smooth and enjoyable stay in this beautiful destination.

Italian Language:

Italian is the official language of Italy, including Sorrento. While many locals in Sorrento may speak English, it's always helpful to learn a few basic Italian phrases.

This shows respect for the local culture and can make interactions more enjoyable.

Simple greetings like "Buongiorno" (Good morning), "Grazie" (Thank you), and "Per favore" (Please) can go a long way in establishing a friendly connection with the locals.

Language Assistance:

If you need assistance with language barriers, tourist information centers and hotels often have multilingual staff who can help with translation and communication. Don't hesitate to ask for their support when needed.

They can provide guidance, recommend places to visit, and offer valuable insights into local customs and traditions.

Language Learning Apps and Phrasebooks:

To enhance your language skills and confidence, consider using language learning apps or carrying a pocket-sized phrasebook.

These resources provide useful phrases and vocabulary that can assist you during your stay.

Practicing a few key phrases can help you navigate daily interactions, such as ordering at restaurants or asking for directions.

Cultural Sensitivity:

Cultural sensitivity plays a crucial role in effective communication. Being respectful of local customs and traditions is important when interacting with the people of Sorrento. Take the time to understand their culture, norms, and etiquette.

For example, it's customary to greet people with a handshake or a kiss on the cheek, known as "bacio sulla guancia," when meeting friends or acquaintances.

Non-Verbal Communication:

Non-verbal communication, such as gestures and body language, can also contribute to effective interaction. Italians are known for their expressive gestures, so observe and learn from the locals.

However, it's important to note that gestures can have different meanings in different cultures, so be mindful of their appropriateness and avoid unintentional misunderstandings.

Local Customs and Courtesy:

Understanding local customs and practicing courtesy is key to fostering positive communication.

For example, it is common to greet shopkeepers and restaurant staff with a friendly "Buongiorno" upon entering an establishment. Remember to use "grazie" (thank you) and "prego" (you're welcome) to express your appreciation and acknowledge assistance received.

Communication Technology:

Stay connected with loved ones back home using communication technology such as Wi-Fi or mobile data. Most hotels, restaurants, and cafes offer internet access, allowing you to communicate through messaging apps, email, or video calls.

It's also advisable to have a mobile translation app handy for quick translations or to assist in communicating specific needs or inquiries.

Common Phrases and Expressions:

When exploring Sorrento, knowing a few common phrases and expressions can enhance your interactions with locals and make your trip more enjoyable. In this section, we will provide you with essential phrases for various situations, helping you navigate the city with ease.

44 Common Expression and Phrases To Connect Like a Pro

Greetings and Basic Phrases:

1. **Buongiorno:** Good morning / Good day
2. **Buonasera:** Good evening
3. **Ciao:** Hello / Goodbye (informal)
4. **Mi chiamo...:** My name is...
5. **Come stai? / Come state?:** How are you? (informal / formal)
6. **Molto bene:** Very well
7. **Grazie:** Thank you
8. **Prego:** You're welcome
9. **Scusa / Scusami:** Excuse me / Sorry (informal)
10. **Per favore:** Please

Ordering Food and Drinks Phrases:

11. **Posso avere il menu, per favore?:** May I have the menu, please?
12. **Vorrei ordinare..., per favore:** I would like to order..., please
13. **Un tavolo per due, per favore:** A table for two, please
14. **Mi consiglia qualcosa di tipico della zona?:** Could you recommend something typical from the region?
15. **Vorrei pagare**: I would like to pay

Asking for Directions Phrases:

16. **Scusi, dov'è...?:** Excuse me, where is...?
17. **Come arrivo a...?:** How do I get to...?
18. **È lontano?:** Is it far?
19. **A sinistra:** To the left
20. **A destra:** To the right
21. **Dritto:** Straight ahead
22. **Qui vicino:** Nearby here

Shopping and Bargaining Phrases:

23. **Quanto costa?:** How much does it cost?

24. **Posso avere uno sconto?:** Can I have a discount?
25. **È troppo caro:** It's too expensive
26. **Posso provarlo?:** Can I try it on?
27. **C'è una taglia diversa?:** Do you have a different size?
28. **Mi piace molto:** I like it a lot

Expressing Gratitude Phrases:

29. **Grazie mille:** Thank you very much
30. **È stato molto gentile:** You have been very kind
31. **Sono molto grato/a:** I am very grateful

Cultural Etiquette Phrases:

32. **Bacio sulla guancia:** Cheek kiss greeting
33. **Si prega di coprire le spalle:** Please cover your shoulders
34. **Si prega di non toccare:** Please do not touch

Emergency Situations:

35. **Aiuto!:** Help!
36. **Ho bisogno di un dottore:** I need a doctor
37. **Dov'è l'ospedale più vicino?:** Where is the nearest hospital?

Expressing Interest Phrases:

38. **Mi piace molto:** I like it a lot
39. **È bellissimo / bellissima:** It's beautiful
40. **Mi piacerebbe visitare:** I would like to visit

Making Friends Phrases:

41. **Posso unirmi a voi?:** May I join you?
42. **Cosa mi consigli di fare qui?:** What do you recommend I do here?
43. **Di dove sei?:** Where are you from?
44. **È un piacere conoscerti:** It's a pleasure to meet you

By familiarizing yourself with these common phrases and expressions, you'll be able to navigate Sorrento with confidence, engage with locals, and immerse yourself in the culture of this charming city.

"Once you've seen Sorrento, you carry it with you wherever you go, for it leaves an indelible mark on your heart."

- Guy de Maupassant

Chapter 11: Essential Information

Before embarking on your journey to Sorrento, it's essential to have the necessary information to ensure a smooth and enjoyable trip.

Currency and Money Matters:

The official currency in Sorrento, as in the rest of Italy, is the Euro (€). It's recommended to have some cash on hand for smaller establishments that may not accept credit cards. ATMs are widely available throughout the city, allowing you to withdraw cash as needed. Major credit cards are generally accepted in hotels, restaurants, and larger stores.

Climate and Weather:

The best time to visit is during the spring (April to June) and fall (September to October) when the weather is pleasant and the tourist crowds are smaller. Summers can be hot, so it's advisable to pack sunscreen, a hat, and lightweight clothing. Don't forget to bring comfortable walking shoes for exploring the city's charming streets.

Transportation:

Sorrento is well-connected to neighboring cities and attractions by various modes of transportation. The Circumvesuviana train provides access to popular destinations like Pompeii, Herculaneum, and Naples. Buses are also available for traveling within the region.

If you plan to explore the Amalfi Coast, consider taking a ferry or hydrofoil from Sorrento's Marina Piccola. Taxis and rental cars are also available for convenient transportation.

Language:

The official language of Sorrento is Italian. While many locals may speak English, it's always helpful to learn a few basic Italian phrases to facilitate communication and show respect for the local culture.

A pocket-sized phrasebook or language app can assist you in navigating daily interactions.

Local Customs and Etiquette:

Respecting local customs and etiquette is important when visiting Sorrento. It's customary to greet people with a friendly "Buongiorno" or "Buonasera" when entering shops, restaurants, or other establishments.

Dress modestly when visiting churches or religious sites, ensuring shoulders and knees are covered. Tipping is not mandatory in Italy, but it's appreciated for exceptional service.

Safety and Emergency Contacts:

Sorrento is generally a safe destination for tourists. However, it's always wise to take standard precautions to safeguard your belongings and personal safety. In case of emergency, dial 112 for general emergencies or 113 for police assistance.

It's advisable to have travel insurance to cover any unforeseen circumstances during your trip.

Local Customs and Culinary Delights:

Sorrento is known for its delicious cuisine and culinary traditions. Don't miss the opportunity to try local specialties such as fresh seafood, and Neapolitan pizza.

Embrace the local customs, such as enjoying a leisurely meal and savoring the flavors of the region's gastronomy.

In a nutshell, by familiarizing yourself with these essential details, you'll be well-prepared to make the most of your visit to Sorrento. Remember to embrace the local culture, respect the customs, and immerse yourself in the enchanting atmosphere of this captivating destination.

Frequently Asked Questions (FAQ)

As you plan your trip to Sorrento, you may have some common questions in mind. In this section, we have compiled a list of frequently asked questions to provide you with the information you need to make the most of your visit to this enchanting destination.

Q: What is the best time to visit Sorrento?

A: The best time to visit Sorrento is during the spring (April to June) and fall (September to October) when the weather is pleasant, and the tourist crowds are smaller. Summers can be hot, so if you prefer fewer crowds and milder temperatures, consider visiting during the shoulder seasons.

Q: How do I get to Sorrento from Naples?

A: Sorrento is easily accessible from Naples. You can take the Circumvesuviana train from Naples Central Station to Sorrento. The journey takes approximately one hour and offers stunning views of the Bay of Naples along the way.

Q: Are credit cards widely accepted in Sorrento?

A: Yes, major credit cards are generally accepted in hotels, restaurants, and larger stores in Sorrento. However, it's always a good idea to carry some cash for smaller establishments that may not accept cards.

Q: What are the must-see attractions in Sorrento?

A: Sorrento is filled with captivating attractions. Some of the must-see spots include the historic center, Piazza Tasso, Marina Grande, Villa Comunale, and the scenic viewpoints overlooking the Bay of Naples. Don't forget to explore the charming streets and indulge in the local cuisine.

Q: Is it safe to drink tap water in Sorrento?

A: Yes, tap water in Sorrento is generally safe to drink. However, if you prefer, you can always opt for bottled water, which is readily available in stores and restaurants.

Q: How can I explore the Amalfi Coast from Sorrento?

A: To explore the Amalfi Coast from Sorrento, you can take a ferry or hydrofoil from Sorrento's Marina Piccola.

These boats will take you to popular destinations such as Positano, Amalfi, and Capri, allowing you to experience the breathtaking beauty of the coastline.

Q: What are the local customs and etiquette I should be aware of?

A: When visiting Sorrento, it's customary to greet people with a friendly "Buongiorno" or "Buonasera" when entering shops, restaurants, or other establishments. Dress modestly when visiting churches or religious sites, ensuring shoulders and knees are covered. Tipping is not mandatory in Italy, but it's appreciated for exceptional service.

Q: Are there any specific cultural events or festivals in Sorrento?

A: Sorrento hosts several cultural events and festivals throughout the year, including the Sorrento Summer Festival and the Sorrento Jazz Festival. These events showcase music, arts, and local traditions, providing visitors with a unique cultural experience.

The Ideal 7-Days Itinerary Plan in Sorrento

In this section, we present an ideal 7-day itinerary that encompasses the best attractions and experiences this enchanting destination has to offer.

Day 1: Arrival and Sorrento City Center

Upon arrival in Sorrento, take some time to settle into your accommodation and soak in the charming atmosphere of the city center. Explore the historic streets, visit Piazza Tasso, and enjoy a leisurely stroll along the scenic waterfront promenade. Indulge in authentic Italian cuisine at one of the local trattorias or restaurants.

Day 2: Pompeii and Mount Vesuvius

Embark on a fascinating journey to the ancient city of Pompeii, a UNESCO World Heritage Site. Explore the remarkably preserved ruins and immerse yourself in the rich history of this once-thriving Roman city. Afterward, venture to the majestic Mount Vesuvius, where you can hike to the summit and marvel at panoramic views of the surrounding landscape.

Day 3: Amalfi Coast Drive

Experience the breathtaking beauty of the Amalfi Coast with a scenic drive along the coastal road. Stop at picturesque towns like Positano, Amalfi, and Ravello, each offering its own unique charm. Admire the colorful houses clinging to cliffs, enjoy the stunning views of the turquoise sea, and savor delicious seafood at a local restaurant.

Day 4: Capri Island

Take a day trip to the captivating island of Capri. Hop on a ferry from Sorrento and explore the island's natural wonders and glamorous atmosphere. Visit the stunning Blue Grotto, take a leisurely walk through the charming streets of Capri Town, and enjoy panoramic views from the Gardens of Augustus. Don't miss the opportunity to indulge in some shopping and savor local delicacies.

Day 5: Sorrento's Gardens and Marina Grande

Spend the day exploring Sorrento's beautiful gardens. Visit the Villa Comunale and stroll through its lush greenery while enjoying stunning views of the Gulf of Naples.

Continue your journey to Marina Grande, a picturesque fishing village with colorful houses and a charming beach. Relax by the sea, savor fresh seafood, and soak in the laid-back coastal ambiance.

Day 6: Day of Relaxation

Take a day to relax and enjoy Sorrento's serene atmosphere. Unwind at one of the stunning beaches along the coast, such as Marina Piccola or Bagni della Regina Giovanna. Alternatively, pamper yourself with a spa treatment or indulge in a leisurely boat trip along the coastline, taking in the scenic beauty of the region.

Day 7: Local Experiences and Farewell

Immerse yourself in Sorrento's local culture by participating in a cooking class, where you can learn the secrets of authentic Italian cuisine. Visit local artisan workshops to witness traditional crafts, such as ceramics and woodwork. Spend your final evening in Sorrento enjoying a romantic sunset at a scenic viewpoint, creating lasting memories of your time in this enchanting destination.

Final Thoughts

As your journey through this travel guide to Sorrento comes to an end, we hope that you have found it informative and inspiring. Sorrento is a destination that captures the hearts of travelers with its breathtaking views, rich history, and warm hospitality.

I hope this travel guide has inspired you to visit Sorrento soon. If you do, I'm sure you'll have a wonderful time.

Here are a few final thoughts to keep in mind as you plan your trip:

- **Cherish the Moments:**

During your time in Sorrento, take a moment to soak in the beauty of your surroundings. Whether you're admiring the sunset over the Bay of Naples, exploring the ancient streets, or savoring the flavors of the local cuisine, remember to pause and appreciate the magical moments that make your visit unforgettable.

- **Immerse Yourself in the Culture:**

Sorrento offers a unique blend of ancient traditions and vibrant contemporary life. Take the opportunity to embrace the local customs, try your hand at some basic Italian phrases, and interact with the friendly locals.

- **Explore Beyond the Guidebook:**

While this travel guide provides you with a comprehensive overview of Sorrento's highlights, don't be afraid to venture off the beaten path. Explore the lesser-known neighborhoods, strike up conversations with locals, and seek out hidden gems that may not be featured in guidebooks.

Leave a Positive Footprint:

As a responsible traveler, it's essential to leave a positive impact on the places you visit. Respect the environment, follow local regulations, and engage in sustainable practices. Support local businesses and artisans, and be mindful of the cultural heritage of the city.

- **Carry the Memories:**

Long after your visit to Sorrento, the memories and experiences you've gained will stay with you. Whether it's the scent of lemons wafting through the streets, the warmth of the sun on your skin, or the laughter shared with newfound friends, hold onto these cherished moments and let them inspire your future adventures.

We hope that this travel guide has provided you with the knowledge and inspiration to embark on a remarkable adventure in Sorrento, where every street corner reveals a new story and every moment becomes a treasure to cherish.

Safe travels, and may your future journeys be filled with the same wonder and delight you've experienced in Sorrento.

Until we meet again,

Dan L. Allbeta

Travel Journal

Travel Budget

	Transportation	Food	Accommodation
Budget			

	Shopping	Subscription	Entertainment
Budget			

Packing Checklist

Packing Checklist

Documents	Clothes	Toiletries

Gadgets	Contacts	Miscellaneous

Travel Itinerary

Travel Itinerary

Day 1

Place To See		
Transportation	Activity	Time

Day 2

Place To See		
Transportation	Activity	Time

Travel Itinerary

Day 3

Place To See		
Transportation	Activity	Time

Day 4

Place To See		
Transportation	Activity	Time

Travel Itinerary

Day 5

Place To See		
Transportation	Activity	Time

Day 6

Place To See		
Transportation	Activity	Time

Travel Itinerary

Day 7

Place To See		
Transportation	Activity	Time

Day 8

Place To See		
Transportation	Activity	Time

Travel Itinerary

Day 9

Place To See		
Transportation	Activity	Time

Day 10

Place To See		
Transportation	Activity	Time

My Notes

My Note

My Note

My Note

My Note

My Note

My Note

My Note

My Note

My Note

My Note

Other Inspiring Travel Companion by the Author

Easy-Peasy Pocket Travel Guide (Travel Series)

https://www.amazon.com/dp/B0CFT9BXP7

Printed in Great Britain
by Amazon